Fragments Within My Orbit

BAROQUE MEDUSA

BookLeaf Publishing

India | USA | UK

Presentation by *BookLeaf Publishing*

Web: www.bookleafpub.com

E-mail: info@bookleafpub.com

ISBN: 9789363304918

First edition 2024

For my Dad, the original writer of the family. I miss you every day. Thank you for teaching me how to dream.

Altitude

Viewpoints from peering eyes
Laments disdain as they criticize
I refuse to conform, I'd rather surprise
My lifestyle is not one to be downsized

Fantasy world that plays out in my head
Started from a thought in which it said,
"My inner child no longer needs to break bread
With those who've grown brain dead"

Determined to bring this fantasy to fruition
I buckle in, no need for permission
Writing my way to the top
Soon to have a following from behind my
desktop
Living out loud, my birthright
A free bird, I take flight

Boom Box

To dream is to love
My passion, a heartbeat
Ups and downs
Murmurs, at times
Ever the loner
Observe from afar

Then you came along

You consume me
Then I tire
The time apart
Brings me back
To missing You

I always have you
In the back of my mind
Or on me
Or tucked in my closet
Track suits and sneakers
Handbags and hoops
Gold chains for drip

There is no love
Like that of ours

Tried & true
You lift me up
Hold me tight
Vibe with me

You are
Old school east coast
Hip Hop

Lana Del Rey

After the sun gets tucked away
I press play
Pour me a double
Locked in to start trouble

Hypnotize you with my grind
We now are forever entwined
Me, in my power
You, hungry to devour

Ultraviolence
Body Electric
Gods and Monsters
Say Yes To Heaven
Money Power Glory

My playlist is that of sovereignty
It is me in my honesty
Don't blame me for my prowess
It's birthed from Lana Del Rey, the lawless

Burnt Amber

Longer days fade to longer nights
The coolness in the morning air
Wraps around me tight
We become the perfect pair

No strangers to the shadows
We don't easily scare
You are mine; nobody knows
Because they won't care

I take refuge in the briefness
Here, only for a season
Nothing between us
Everything within reason

Your potent stillness
Provides me with peace
Others cry illness
Halt and cease

Thank you Fall
For giving me your all
Autumn isn't for most
To this, I toast

Hoodie SEAZN

6

Just looking at you
Brings me comfort, coziness
When I put you on
The girly comes out in me
Need to be held close, cuddled

Altered Perception

Daily illusions
Swapped to vibrant colors, sounds
Nature's caps and stems
Our relationship, still new
Walls broken, heart now open

Lunas

What is it about you?
New or Full
When you are impending
Insomnia ensues

My mind, a melting pot
Ideas, loves, tasks
Your feminine energy
Won't lay them to bed

Invisible or illuminated
Regardless of phase,
I love you
Please let me rest

Orion

You're my favorite
Out of all the constellations
Easiest to see
Adonis belt, prominent
Desired hunter

Seven Rings of Solitude

Of all the rings,
Yours are the finest
The seven that enclose you
Shelter you in place
Isolated from it all

Seen with the naked eye
Aloof, dormant
Standoffish to most
Yet a force to be reckoned with

Ruler of the sea goats
It's no wonder you and I
Get along quite well

For I, too, thrive in isolation
My thoughts, front and center
For me to dissect
Now one with my thoughts
As the world passes by

Java

I take my first sip
Your complex embodiment
Greets me with a kiss
Senses come into focus
Mornings with you, complete bliss

Marine Layer

In the mornings, when you appear
Reminders of my coastal life
Riding with you above
My thoughts ascend
As I speak them out loud

You bring me comfort
When they're echoed back
Your blanket of protection
Sets the somber tone, tucked in

With the sun and its routine,
You slowly give in
A sign of defeat
I say goodbye
Hoping it won't be for long

SoCal Coastline

Oceanic blue
Comes to meet copper tone grains
Add in, salty air
Beauty, there for the taking
The SoCal coast, sacrosanct

The Pacific

Sand beneath me
Sun's out, must see
Salty air for me to breathe
Not one to grit my teeth

Coastal living, my domain
Inland dwelling, for the lame
I shall soon return
Not yet my turn

Number's almost up
Almost time for my close up
The Pacific, another true love
It fits me like a glove

Imminent Icon

My moves, intentional
Burn bridges that no longer serve
This may sound unconventional
To your optic nerve

The magic I possess
I no longer suppress
An icon in the making
At times, heartbreaking

I've raised the bar
To walk with the Moon and Stars
I am now a celestial being
In harmony with the supreme being

Microdots

Once your magic takes hold,
My mind slows its grind
Sensory, awakened
Front and center

In the stillness,
Not a care in the world
Except to be in the moment,
Observe
Appreciate the space I'm in
With you holding my hand

A Letter

Hi Dad,

Remembering when you'd come home
Picked me up and held me in your arms
With Frank Sinatra on the airwaves

Your depiction of a gentleman
Engraved in my head
Few have stepped to the plate
I've found one…

With you as my angel now,
Send him to me
It's his turn to press play
And take my hand to dance

VANILLA GORILLA

Do you think of me
As much as I think you?
Primal desires

Chopper

Let's drop everything
Get on your bike
Ride until the tires melt off
Nothing else matters

HIM

In my thoughts again
Eyes closed to see you see me
I long for your touch
I want more of you, of us
You take the lead, I follow

Ready

To my Gorilla:
I've changed my mind. I want more.
Be monogamous

A Matter of Time

We have come so far
Don't tell me I'm not 'The One'
I'm yours, forever